© 2003 White-Thomson Publishing Ltd

White-Thomson Publishing Ltd,
2-3 St Andrew's Place, Lewes,
East Sussex BN7 1UP

Published in Great Britain in 2003 by Hodder
Wayland, an imprint of Hodder Children's
Books

This book was produced for White-Thomson
Publishing Ltd by Ruth Nason.

Design: Carole Binding
Picture research: Glass Onion Pictures

The right of Sarah Lennard-Brown to be
identified as the author of this work has been
asserted by her in accordance with the
Copyright, Designs and Patents Act 1988.

British Library Cataloguing in Publication Data
Lennard-Brown, Sarah
  Autism. - (Health Issues)
  1. Autism - Juvenile literature
  I. Title
  616.8'982

ISBN 0 7502 4370 8

Printed in Hong Kong

Hodder Children's Books
A division of Hodder Headline Limited
338 Euston Road, London NW1 3BH

Acknowledgements

The author and publishers thank the following for their permission to reproduce photographs and
illustrations: Martyn Chillmaid: pages 9, 43, 48, 53; Corbis Images: pages 5 (Lou Cypher), 21 (Tom
Stewart Photography), 23b (Bettmann); Ferdinand Hamburger Archives of The Johns Hopkins
University: page 6; Angela Hampton Family Life Picture Library: pages 11t, 12, 15, 26, 28, 34, 49,
57; Photofusion (David Montford): page 59; Popperfoto: pages 33, 44, 51; Science Photo Library:
pages 4 (GJLP-CNRI), 7 (BSIP, Beranger), 30 (Department of Clinical Radiology, Salisbury District
Hospital), 35 (Lowell Georgia); Topham ImageWorks: pages 3, 11b, 19, 24, 36, 41, 54; Topham
Picturepoint: cover and pages 1, 23t, 38; Stephen Wiltshire/John Johnson (Authors' Agent) Ltd: page
17. The photographs on pages 29, 45 and 58 are from the Hodder Wayland Picture Library. The
illustrations on pages 31, 32, 42 and 47 are by Carole Binding.

Thanks also to Tiffany Brown, Gwen Cook and Sonja McGurk for their invaluable help with research
for the book.

Note: Photographs illustrating the case studies in this book were posed by models.

Contents

Introduction
A spectrum disorder

Autism is a very complex disorder which affects the way a person experiences and interacts with the world around them. It does not affect a person's appearance; you cannot tell if someone has autism by looking at them. People with autism view the world in a different way from people who are not autistic. Sometimes this is described as 'dancing to a different beat' or 'living in their own world'. For people with autism the world is a confusing place full of sounds, sights and smells that are hard to understand and make sense of. Being autistic can help people be very creative and original, to 'think outside the box'. However, autism can also make it very hard to make friends, or get on with other people, or cope with everyday living.

Autism is a spectrum disorder, which means that the disorder affects people in a range of ways, from just slightly to very severely. Some people with autism live normal lives and manage very well, often not even realizing that some of the things they experience or do are due to autism. People with high-functioning autism or Asperger's syndrome can be found in many areas of society. They learn to use their intellect to 'blend in' socially, and they find careers that use their abilities. However, some people with autism need constant care and supervision. Some people with autism never learn to talk or communicate. They seem to be locked in their own world, with no desire to reach out and contact other people.

Causes
Recent research has shown that autistic behaviour is linked to changes in brain structure, but the causes of autism are not yet fully understood.

Every society and country around the world has people with autism. It is not affected by race, ethnic group or religion. The only difference is that it seems to affect boys more than girls. About four times as many boys are affected by autism as girls.

Valuing uniqueness

Autism is permanent. It does not go away and there is no cure. However, there are strategies and therapies that can help people with autism to cope with their problems. Many adults with autism would not change. They value the unique view of the world that autism gives them and enjoy life to the full.

People are gradually becoming more aware of the needs of autistic people. In this book, we start by trying to understand what autism is all about. We then look at high-functioning autism and Asperger's syndrome, and how these affect people. The causes of autism are not yet properly understood. In Chapter 3 we look at current research and theories and discuss the controversies sparked by autism throughout history. As with most conditions, people with autism can be helped by various therapies and strategies, especially if these are started early enough. In Chapter 4 we investigate some of these therapies and examine their effectiveness. Living with autism has its ups and downs, both for the individual with autism and for their family and friends. These issues are discussed in Chapter 5.

No outward sign

You cannot tell if someone has autism just by looking at them.

1 What is autism?
Dancing to a different beat

Autism was first recognized in the 1940s by two people working in different places at the same time: Hans Asperger, in Austria, and Leo Kanner, in the USA. Both men described a group of children who had:

- problems with speech, communication and imagination;
- an intense focus on certain objects or occupations;
- excellent visual abilities;
- an extreme dislike of change.

Both men gave the disorder the same name, autism, which comes from a Greek word meaning 'self'.

Leo Kanner
Leo Kanner's work on autism became best known in the English-speaking world.

Although the condition wasn't recognized by doctors until the twentieth century, there are many stories from throughout history of people displaying autistic behaviour. Some people think that tales of 'changeling children' were explanations for children with autism. According to these stories, fairies would take a human child and leave a beautiful 'changeling' or fairy child in its place. The 'changelings' were said to grow up remote from other people and 'in a world of their own', a good description of autism.

Autism is one of a group of disorders known as Pervasive Developmental Disorders or PDD. Pervasive Developmental Disorders involve problems with speech, communication and getting on with other people (social interaction), as well as repetitive and compulsive behaviours. Autism can involve all of these problems to varying degrees, or just a few. Autism is a 'spectrum disorder'. At one end of the spectrum are people with very few noticeable autistic problems; the problems may be so mild that the person is never actually diagnosed as autistic. In the middle of the spectrum people may be diagnosed with high-functioning autism or Asperger's syndrome. The other end of the spectrum is sometimes called classic autism, and people with this degree of disability may take many years to communicate with other people or may never learn to do so.

Estimates of the numbers of people affected by autism vary widely. One of the most reliable puts the level of people with an autistic spectrum disorder at 91 people out of every 10,000: that is nearly 1 per cent of the general population. This is thought to be true for every country, race, religion and ethnic group around the world. The only group of people less likely to be affected by autism are girls. It seems that for every four boys with an autistic spectrum disorder there is only one girl. Why this should be so is a mystery, like many aspects of autism. One possible reason is that it may be more difficult to recognize autism in girls. Another suggestion (from Hans Asperger) is that autism is an extreme form of 'male' behaviour and so it may naturally occur more in boys than girls.

Every person with autism is an individual and each individual's personality has a big impact on the way autism shows itself. This means that every person with autism is different, and so when people talk about the behaviours associated with autism they tend to talk in general terms. The way one person responds to autistic problems is different from the way another responds.

Boys and girls
There are thought to be approximately four boys with an autistic spectrum disorder to every one girl.

All people with an autistic spectrum disorder have similar problems with three specific areas: social relationships, verbal and non-verbal communication, and imagination. These are often known as the triad of impairment.

Social relationships

For people with autism, social relationships can be terrifying and confusing. To be successful at relating to other people and 'getting on' with them, you need to understand how they are feeling, what they expect to happen and the social rules that apply to the situation you are in. People who are not autistic do not usually have to learn these things. They pick them up naturally as they develop through childhood. People who are not autistic do not even think about these matters; they are so much a part of life that they are almost like breathing – you just do it.

'I find it very difficult being with more than two other people. I don't know what I'm supposed to do or say!'
(Darius, aged 16)

For example, if you are at a friend's house and you want a drink of water, you have to know the social rules that apply. Who is the right person to ask: your friend or his parents? How close do you stand to the person you ask and what words do you use? The distance and the degree of politeness depend on whom you are asking. Does it matter if you slurp or glug, or the water drips down your chin? What do you do with the glass when you've finished? Is it appropriate to burp and, if you do, what do you say or do afterwards? All these are issues that non-autistic people know about and deal with, without thinking. But if you have an autistic spectrum disorder, you have to consciously learn and remember social rules like these.

Problems with social relationships

People with autism find it difficult to:

- ⚙ *understand the social rules that people follow when they interact;*
- ⚙ *understand how other people think or feel;*
- ⚙ *work out when they are being taken advantage of;*
- ⚙ *make friends;*
- ⚙ *interact with other people;*
- ⚙ *play games;*
- ⚙ *be part of a team.*

Some people describe autism as being born without a social 'sixth sense'. Some autistic people never realize that there are social rules and really don't care if there are. Others become aware that there are rules, but they don't know or understand them. Their actions may be considered odd, rude, naughty, or insulting, although this was not what the person meant.

People with autism may appear indifferent to other people. They may be very formal, sticking rigidly to the rules they have learnt about social relationships, no matter what situation they are in. They find it hard to understand other people's thoughts and feelings and sometimes don't even realize that other people have their own thoughts and feelings. They can also be very trusting and naïve, and this can make them vulnerable to people who may wish to take advantage of them or ridicule or bully them.

'Why can't people be logical and consistent? If they just kept the rules the same, I could manage, but they keep on changing them for no reason.'
(Fatima, aged 14)

Too close for comfort

When someone stands too close to you it can make you feel very uncomfortable.

Verbal and non-verbal communication

To communicate our thoughts and feelings to others, and to understand other people, we use words (this is verbal communication) and also 'non-verbal' things such as tone of voice and body language. 80 per cent of the information we receive when we talk to a person can come from non-verbal communication, such as the emphasis put on parts of a word, voice control and eye contact.

Speech development can be severely impaired in autistic children. Some people with autism never learn to speak at all. Some learn to speak and then just stop speaking; they become mute. Some children can sing or hum beautifully, or accurately mimic machine or animal noises, but cannot speak. Some children with autism learn to speak fairly normally but have other problems with language, which can be very difficult to work out.

People with autism can also have difficulties understanding speech. They can find it very difficult to organize the sounds they hear into recognizable patterns. It can take them a while to work out what you have said. Occasionally they may hear parts of words run together, which makes the words meaningless. Also people with autism tend to take language literally: they believe each word is fact. For example, a figure of speech like 'crying your eyes out' will be frightening for an autistic child who may well believe that, if you cry, your eyes will fall out.

Problems with communication

Autistic people can find it difficult to:

- *develop speech;*
- *understand changes in meaning of words depending on how they are said ;*
- *understand speech;*
- *use language to communicate;*
- *understand body language;*
- *have eye contact with other people;*
- *take turns in conversations.*

'If I ask Dan to "Wait a minute", he stands and watches the clock until exactly one minute has gone by. He doesn't understand that I want him to wait for me to finish what I am doing.' (Sue, mum)

People who do not have an autistic spectrum disorder do not normally give a second thought to the way they communicate with other people. They just get on with it. They expect other people to be able to tell that they are feeling cross or sad or happy, from the expression on their face. This is not always the case for people with autism. Autistic people often have problems making eye contact with other people, especially if they are anxious or distressed (which can be a lot of the time). This means that they do not concentrate on your face when they are talking to you and so they tend not to notice when they are boring you or being irritating.

People with autism also tend not to produce facial expressions. Complex emotions such as confusion, enquiry or concern may not show on their faces. This can make them appear wooden and uncaring and can place a strain on relationships.

Autistic people seem to take in their whole environment in one go. They are surrounded by sounds, smells, tastes, textures, sights, colour and light. The world can feel as if it is bombarding their senses with things to take in all at the same time.

Expressions
Do you know how these people are feeling?

Imagination

Your imagination is important in helping you to communicate with other people. For example, you need to be able to use your imagination to sympathize with someone who has lost their mobile phone. If you had no imagination, you would not be able to 'put yourself in their shoes' (another saying that would probably confuse a person with autism – why would you want to wear another person's shoes?). In order to sympathize with another person, you have to be able to imagine how they feel, and then imagine how, if you were in their place, other people's responses to the problem could make you feel better or worse. People with autism do not automatically imagine how other people feel. Some people with autism do not even understand that other people have feelings; others learn that other people have feelings but they understand them on a logical level rather than reacting naturally and instinctively, as most non-autistic people do. This can make autistic people appear remote, wooden and uncaring.

Let's pretend
An important stage in children's development is when they become able to imagine, for example, that the back of a sofa is a train. A child with autism would have difficulty using their imagination in this way.

Problems with imagination show themselves in other ways too. Children with autism often play differently from children of the same age who are not autistic. Play is a very important part of growing and developing. Children need to play in order to learn about the world around them. They start by picking up objects and exploring the sensations they get from them, their sound, taste, texture, colour, smell and movement. Then they begin to use objects, for example, shaking a rattle or rolling a ball. As they get older, they start to use their imaginations and pretend that objects are different things: for instance, pretending a stick is a gun, or a doll is a real person. They learn that if you hide a toy under a blanket, it still exists, and that if you move mum's keys when she has gone out of the room, she will expect them to be where she left them when she returns. This is very important because it means that the child learns that other people have a different point of view from their own; they are separate people, not objects. Pretend games help children learn to think about how other people might feel in different situations. Learning to imagine other people's viewpoints is called developing a theory of mind.

'Ling didn't like pretending when young. The only thing he ever pretended to be was a washing machine. He used to stand in a corner and wave his hands, being a washing machine for hours.'
(Michael, dad)

The development of a theory of mind depends upon brain function and development. If the necessary brain structures do not develop properly, then imaginative play will not occur. Some children with autism do seem to act imaginary play situations but these are often based on things they have seen on TV or in real life. Many children with autism become obsessed with a particular television show or video and watch it repeatedly. Although they may be able to quote the whole show perfectly with the right accent, they often do not understand the story. They can find it hard to follow stories and may take them literally.

Problems with imagination

People with autism find it hard to:

⦿ *understand other people's points of view;*

⦿ *understand that other people are people rather than objects;*

⦿ *develop imaginative play.*

Routines

People with autism usually have routines and special interests, which are repetitive and reassuring. At a basic level, these repetitive actions involve stimulating the senses. Examples are rocking, tasting, chewing, staring at the washing in the washing machine, listening to mechanical noises, or spinning round and round. Sometimes these behaviours can be harmful, but usually only if the individual is frustrated or distressed. These sorts of repetitive actions can last into adult life for the most severely affected people.

'When my sister was young, she would spend hours spinning on the spot or waving her hands round and round. She's nine now and she still likes things that keep rotating.'
(Michaela, aged 13)

Repetitive routines vary depending on the individual. They can involve ordering objects in rows, collecting objects, or having set routines for daily events such as getting dressed or going to bed. Such set routines, which are often based on numbers or music, must be followed exactly every time: for example, everything must be done in even numbers, such as steps, kisses or even eating. Videos are also often the focus of repetitive routines. They are especially treasured as they repeat the same sounds and words over and over

An obsession with buses

My brother drives me crazy. He's got this thing about buses. He can tell you what sort of bus it is, even if he just sees its rear light. It was OK for the first two months – I could pretend to be interested – but now, as soon as he starts on about buses, I just want to scream. He even watches videos about buses, not just once a day; sometimes he watches one again and again and again. I counted that one day he watched the same video ten times, back to back. He was even talking about taping bus sounds so that he could listen to them as he falls asleep. At least I don't have to share a room with him. It's so boring and he never notices when I've had enough. Mum sometimes asks me to talk to him about buses because he's having a bad day. Why should I? It's enough to give me a bad day! No one has to listen to me talking about my favourite things. I know he has autism and I ought to be kind, but what about being kind to me!
(Louise, aged 16)

with no variation. Interrupting these routines in any way can result in tantrums and distress. Tantrums can be a particular problem for people with autism.

For people with high-functioning autism or Asperger's syndrome these routines can appear as an obsession or fascination with a particular subject: for example, train-spotting, space missions, Lego, dinosaurs. These routines and special interests are often a way of trying to get a grip on the world. They are reassuring and calming.

Sensory sensitivity

The world is a confusing and frightening place for people with autism. They often experience touch, taste, smell, sight and sound very intensely. They can be rapidly over-whelmed and frightened by sounds that would not distress other people. Many people with autism dislike being touched because they can experience even the lightest touch as painful. Others love heavy pressure. They may not seem to experience pain, and this can result in them having quite serious injuries, or painful infections, that they do not tell anyone about. Many people with autism are also very sensitive to the texture of the clothes they are wearing or to the tastes and textures of foods.

Video control
People with autism often like to watch the same video over and over again.

People with autism tend to rely heavily on their ability to see things. The world comes at them in great waves of experience, sights, sounds, smells, tastes and sensations. It is very confusing. They find it hard to sort through all this information about the world around them and to make sense of it. One result of this can be that they retreat to something safe, such as a special interest or routine.

They can appear deaf or 'in their own world', concentrating single-mindedly on the object of their interest. Some people with autism, having learnt to talk, simply stop doing so. It is as if they have opted out of attempting to communicate with the world.

Movement

Many children and adults with autism display certain types of movements. These can include rocking, hand flapping, jumping up and down, making strange faces or dancing on the spot. The movements often happen when the person is excited, distressed or anxious or has seen something that fascinates them. If they are absorbed in an activity that interests them, the movements tend to disappear.

Some people with autism, especially those with high-functioning autism or Asperger's syndrome, tend to be clumsy. The clumsiness tends to come and go, being more severe when the person feels over-stimulated or anxious. Some children with an autistic disorder can be very agile and are afraid of nothing.

People with autism often have lax joints (sometimes called being double-jointed). This means that they are very flexible, but it can make it hard for them to control their movements. Most children with autism have great trouble with sports and games. Coordinating movement at the same time as remembering all the social rules of a game can be overwhelmingly difficult. These children tend to prefer solitary repetitive activities such as swimming, cycling and trampolining.

Anxiety

Anxiety and special fears are also problems in the lives of many children with autism. They can become extremely anxious in situations they do not understand or where unusual things happen.

'I feel funny when things are different. I don't like things changing. I like things to be normal.'
(Toni, aged 9)

Children with autism often do not respond to experiences that you would expect to upset them. They can respond

inappropriately, laughing when someone is hurt, for example. This is not from rudeness but often because they simply cannot put themselves in someone else's position and work out the right way to respond. Conversely, things that other people would not worry about can be devastating for an autistic person: for example, a machine not working properly, alarms, particular colours, or even everyday objects such as hot-air hand-dryers in public toilets.

Special skills

Some people with autism have special skills; they may be superb artists, excellent musicians, or amazing engineers. A person with autism tends to have differing levels of ability at different skills. For example, they may be very good with numbers but unable to read. Some people with autism also have learning disabilities. Those with high-functioning autism or Asperger's syndrome often have normal intelligence levels and a proportion of them are gifted (highly intelligent). In the next chapter, we will look at high-functioning autism and Asperger's syndrome in more detail.

Los Angeles

The artist Stephen Wiltshire is an 'autistic savant', a severely autistic person with one amazing talent. His photographic memory enables him to draw perfectly accurate representations of city and architectural scenes.

2 Asperger's and high-functioning autism

Asperger's syndrome and high-functioning autism are the names given to conditions that affect a distinct group of people on the autistic spectrum. These people tend to be clever, with an average or above-average intelligence level, but they still show the triad of impairment (pages 8-13).

Social relationships

People with high-functioning autism and Asperger's syndrome find social interaction difficult. They find it hard to interpret facial expressions and learn the social rules that people without autism take for granted. This can make it difficult for them to make and keep friends. However, unlike most people with autism, people with Asperger's syndrome actually want to make friends. They often feel lonely and want to make social contact.

Verbal and non-verbal communication

People with Asperger's syndrome and high-functioning autism can speak fluently. They often use complex words, though they do not always understand their meaning. Their speech usually develops normally but they are often very formal and precise in the way they speak. For example, an 8-year old girl with Asperger's syndrome referred to a classmate as 'that nice young man'.

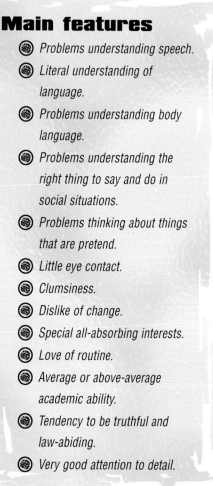

Main features

- Problems understanding speech.
- Literal understanding of language.
- Problems understanding body language.
- Problems understanding the right thing to say and do in social situations.
- Problems thinking about things that are pretend.
- Little eye contact.
- Clumsiness.
- Dislike of change.
- Special all-absorbing interests.
- Love of routine.
- Average or above-average academic ability.
- Tendency to be truthful and law-abiding.
- Very good attention to detail.

They can love talking about their special interests but fail to notice when the person they are talking to becomes bored. They also take language literally. Sayings like 'You'll laugh your head off' can be very frightening to a person with Asperger's syndrome. Jokes can also present problems, unless they are visual; slapstick comedy is often a great favourite.

'These children have very complex language problems. Because of their problems understanding the world from another person's perspective, they often give very little information and so it's hard to grasp what they are talking about.'
(Kira, speech therapist)

Imagination

People with high-functioning autism and Asperger's syndrome tend to prefer things to be real. They usually like data, science and maths, but are not so keen on made-up stories or ideas that you cannot prove, such as religion or philosophy. When they are children they may well play in what appears a normal imaginative way, but a closer look often reveals that they are actually re-enacting situations they have seen on television or in life and they will often go over the same situation again and again.

People with high-functioning autism and Asperger's syndrome dislike change. They usually immerse themselves in special interests like trains, cartoon characters, timetables or machines.

No problem
Maths is often a favourite subject for people with autism.

Age of diagnosis

High-functioning autism and Asperger's syndrome differ from classic autism in the age at which they are diagnosed. Classic autism is usually diagnosed at a young age, when it is noticed that the child is not learning to speak. However, speech develops normally in children with high-functioning autism and Asperger's syndrome and so these conditions often do not become noticeable until the child is older. The average age of diagnosis of Asperger's syndrome is around 7 years old. It is often when a child starts school that the delay in development of social skills is noticed by people outside the family.

Clumsiness

Between 50 and 90 per cent of people with Asperger's syndrome have problems coordinating their movements. They are often very flexible, which can mean that they are very good at getting into some of the more difficult Yoga positions (as long as they don't need to balance at the same time), but they can find it hard to ride a bike or catch a ball. Problems with coordinating movements can also mean that they tend to bang into things or people, especially when they are anxious. These problems tend to come and go with the person's own rhythm or depending on their anxiety levels. One day they may not bump into other people at all, but the next they may be 'all over the place'.

'I hate doing games at school, especially ones that involve catching a ball. I hate people laughing when I want to catch it. I hate the noise and I worry that someone will run into me.' (Alison, aged 16)

Problems with coordination can affect the way a person runs or walks. They may hold their arms awkwardly and move stiffly. This can lead to teasing from people who do not understand. The person may also have problems balancing, and some people with Asperger's syndrome have trouble coordinating both hands to use cutlery or do up buttons.

Difficulty with coordinating fine (that is, delicate or small) movements can cause problems with handwriting. However, one advantage of Asperger's syndrome or high-functioning

Concentration

People with Asperger's or high-functioning autism may concentrate for hours, perfecting a skill.

autism is that you can concentrate for hours at a time on a task you are interested in. Therefore people with these conditions often practise until they become highly skilled at an activity that involves a high degree of coordination, such as drawing or making Lego models, and this can lead to an improvement in their fine movement coordination. However, it does not always work this way, as one of the major problems of autism is that skills learnt in one situation are not easily transferred to another. An individual may be very skilled at making complex small drawings but still have unreadable handwriting.

Anxiety

Anxiety can be a big problem for people with high-functioning autism and Asperger's syndrome. Sensory overload can make them anxious, as can being in a social situation and not knowing the rules. The world often does not obey the rules and can be a very confusing and frightening place. When they are anxious or becoming overloaded, people with high-functioning autism and Asperger's syndrome sometimes make strange noises or movements. These can appear odd to other people, but they are part of the individual's coping mechanism. People with these conditions are often bullied and teased at school because other people see them as different. This makes the anxiety worse and can make school unbearable for them.

'My brother Jack has a hard time at school. Just being there makes him anxious and when he's anxious he makes screeching noises and rocks back and forth. Some kids deliberately wind him up, for a laugh. It's sick.' (Sam, aged 16)

The same or different?

The relationship between high-functioning autism and Asperger's syndrome is very complicated. Some experts in autism think they are the same condition. Others see them as separate but similar. In the 1940s, when Leo Kanner in the USA and Hans Asperger in Austria were separately investigating autism, Kanner's group of patients tended to show learning disabilities and the more obvious signs of classic autism. He published his papers in English and they gained respect in English-speaking countries. Asperger's group of patients included more able people who expressed their autism in different ways. Asperger published his findings in German, also to great acclaim, and his work became well-known in Europe but did not spread to the English-speaking world.

Asperger felt that he and Kanner had discovered separate but similar conditions. However, as more people began to investigate autism, it gradually became apparent that autism is a spectrum disorder. In 1981 Lorna Wing used the term 'Asperger's syndrome' to describe a group of people with autism who were 'more able' academically. Since then, people have become more aware of the condition.

'I have high-functioning autism. I think it is very different to Asperger's, the main point being that I have no desire to make friends.' (Carole, aged 16)

There is still debate about whether Asperger's syndrome and high-functioning autism are different conditions. Some people feel that coordination problems are more common with Asperger's syndrome, though some people with high-functioning autism also have such problems. Another difference is seen in the approach to social interaction. People with Asperger's syndrome want to reach out and communicate with others, to make friends, whereas people with high-functioning autism may not.

Despite this debate, the same therapies are used to help people with high-functioning autism, Asperger's syndrome and classic autism. People with high-functioning autism and Asperger's syndrome are usually clever. The one thing that really affects whether a person with autism will be able to adapt and live a 'normal' lifestyle seems to be intelligence. The cleverer the individual is, the more positive the likely outcome.

Intelligence

Autism is a spectrum disorder. People can have autistic tendencies but not display enough of the symptoms to be classified as autistic. This is especially true for those on the edge of Asperger's syndrome and high-functioning autism. These people are often very intelligent and focused on their chosen interest, and they use their autistic qualities to excel at what they do. It has been said that, in order to excel in any subject, you need some degree of autism. It enables you to think originally, to be creative and unhampered by social conventions about what is possible, and to see things as they are. Many famous artists, scientists and mathematicians may have had Asperger's syndrome or high-functioning autism. It has been suggested that Vincent van Gogh, Albert Einstein and the philosopher Ludwig Wittgenstein may have had Asperger's syndrome.

Vincent van Gogh
'Self-portrait in front of the Easel', 1888.
The artist Vincent van Gogh worked obsessively at his painting and created powerful and original works.

Albert Einstein
Albert Einstein was one of the greatest thinkers of the twentieth century. His ideas contributed to great advances in physics and mathematics. He is especially famous for his theory of relativity.

People with high-functioning autism and Asperger's syndrome may not do well in intelligence tests, even though they are very able. This is because most intelligence tests look at a person's ability across a large number of areas and then give an average score. People with high-functioning autism and Asperger's syndrome tend to be exceptionally good in some areas and not so good in others. In many intelligence tests, the exceptionally good performance can be cancelled out by the not-so-good performance and the person's talents may not show up.

Visual thinking

Another feature of people with Asperger's syndrome and high-functioning autism is that they often think in pictures. This is called visual thinking and it can be very creative. Albert Einstein thought in pictures – he developed his theory of relativity by thinking about boxcars travelling along a light beam. Someone who uses this method of thinking can find it hard to learn in a normal classroom where the teaching mostly relies on speech and written language. Also, students with autism can find it difficult to process all the information from the sounds, tastes, smells and textures that bombard them in a normal classroom. They often find it much easier to learn if information is presented to them visually in a quiet, calm environment.

In class

Classrooms can be challenging places for people with autism. They are full of people and sounds, which can make it very hard to understand what is going on.

Memory and rigid thinking

People with high-functioning autism and Asperger's syndrome tend to have superb long-term memories. They can often remember in detail things that happened in their childhood and information about their special subjects. However, they often have problems remembering things related to speech, such as messages. They also often display rigid thinking. This means that it can be very hard to deflect them from a particular idea or action, for example examining a new computer in someone else's house.

'I find it a bit hard to remember messages. I'm not deaf. It's just that I find it hard to remember things that people have said. Mum gets cross because I forget to give her telephone messages.'
(Harry, aged 14)

Variability

One of the main features of high-functioning autism and Asperger's syndrome is their variability. On a good day the conditions hardly affect a person at all. On a bad day things can be very difficult. Often people with these conditions try very hard to suppress the fear and anxiety they feel at school or with strangers, and will then explode with the tension when they get home. This can make it very difficult for their family, who experience tantrums and huge anxiety at home.

My life with Mr Bean

'It's OK really, Asperger's. I mean, it's not OK being with other people and the noise, but when I'm on my own, watching videos, it's all right. I really like the things I like. I really like Mr Bean videos at the moment. I've got all of them – they really make me laugh. My favourite days are when Mum lets me stay in pyjamas all day and watch videos and work on the computer – I like that too. Worst days are when I have to go to school and do PE. I can't do it and the children laugh at me. I stay in the library at break times. I like my room – it's cosy and I know where everything is – and my videos. I wish I could stay there all the time and not go out. I don't like it when people shout at me – why do they shout? They're not supposed to shout. Mr Bean doesn't shout, but everyone shouts at him, but quietly because there are no words. Mr Bean is excellent.'
(Philip, aged 13)

Conditions that may look like autism

There are several conditions that are similar to autism and are sometimes mistaken for it.

Fragile X syndrome

This syndrome is rare and found mostly in males. It is caused by an abnormality on the X chromosome which results in long face shape, large ears, learning difficulties, over-sensitivity to sound and touch, repetitive movements and routines, hyperactivity, poor eye contact and abnormal speech. This condition is different from autism in that people with Fragile X syndrome tend to avoid other people because of anxiety and dislike of bodily contact, whereas people with autism tend to be indifferent to other people.

Retts syndrome

This rare syndrome, found mainly in girls, is caused by a gene mutation and its effects are severe. Children with Retts syndrome develop normally for 12 to 18 months but then they gradually lose the ability to coordinate their hands. Their head growth slows or stops, walking is difficult and the child may develop a curvature of the spine. Children with Retts often become very anxious and withdrawn, with learning difficulties and poor language skills. Few people with Retts syndrome live to adulthood. Because of the lack of early social skills, many children with Retts syndrome are diagnosed as autistic at the beginning of the condition.

Attention deficit disorder

Attention deficit disorder is sometimes confused with autism. Children with attention deficit disorder (hyperactivity) have difficulty concentrating and other children may not want to play with them. However, this is usually because they don't want to be associated with someone who is likely to be naughty, and not because of social skills

Tantrums

Children with Tourette's syndrome, attention deficit disorder and autistic spectrum disorders are prone to tantrums.

problems. Attention deficit disorder is a separate condition but it can occur with autistic spectrum disorders.

Tourette's syndrome

Tourette's syndrome can also occur with autistic spectrum disorders and has some similar signs. Most people know of Tourette's syndrome as the 'swearing syndrome', where sufferers have an uncontrollable urge to shout swear words in public. In fact, only a small number of Tourette's sufferers have such a severe version of the syndrome. Most experience an uncontrollable urge to make noises and tics or twitches. These are repetitive and not under the control of the individual. They can be suppressed sometimes for a little while but eventually they come out – often more so when the person is stressed. People with Tourette's syndrome often have a quick temper. People with autistic spectrum disorders also often produce strange noises and repetitive movements and are prone to temper tantrums. Sometimes it can be difficult to tell when these signs become Tourette's syndrome.

Socially challenged

In the past, autistic problems were often wrongly diagnosed as mental illness. Autism is not a mental health problem, although it can occur with some mental health problems. Autistic disorders involve a delay in normal development of social and communication skills. Therefore 'socially challenged' or 'socially disabled' are more accurate terms for people with autism.

Deprivation

Autistic-type behaviours are also shown by children who have been deprived of attention, stimulation and loving care. The difference for these children is that, as soon as they start receiving the care that has been lacking, they begin to develop normally. By contrast, children with autistic disorders learn social and communication skills very slowly despite years of tender loving care.

In the next chapter, we shall investigate the mechanisms and controversies relating to the causes of autistic spectrum disorders.

3 The causes of autism
Investigations and controversies

The causes of autism are not completely understood, but recent research into brain structure and function has shown that autistic behaviour is directly linked to changes in brain structure. Developments in genetics are beginning to track down the relationship between genes and autism, and research is also underway to see if exposure to chemicals 'switches on' autistic behaviour. Research into all these areas is at an early stage and there are many controversies, new and old, over the causes of autism.

Happy family
The causes of autism are nothing to do with the way a child is looked after. Most children with autism come from loving families.

Changing ideas

In the 1950s, people commented on the similarities between children with autism and children kept in social isolation. They concluded that autism was caused by cold mothers who neglected their children. This idea was rapidly dismissed for two reasons. Firstly, it was obvious that most autistic children came from loving, caring families. Secondly, as we saw on page 27, children deprived of emotional and social care rapidly develop once such care is provided, whereas children with autism show very slow progress even with intensive loving support.

For a while, the idea that autism was caused by the parents' neglect led to many autistic children being removed from their families and placed in foster homes, to see if changing their environment would help improve their condition. Very little change was observed and the practice was stopped. However, unfortunately, the idea that parents are in some way to blame for their children's autism has still not completely gone away. This can be very upsetting for families already under enormous stress. Thankfully, recent developments in medicine and genetics mean that no intelligent person would consider that autism is a result of parental neglect.

Courage at the supermarket

'Going out with my daughter can be really difficult. Other people don't understand. All they see is a child who looks fine behaving badly, or being rude. They don't understand that Jenny doesn't understand them. In the supermarket, for example, the music, bright lights, noisy people, smells, colours and shapes become too much for her. She starts off OK but is quickly overwhelmed. But she doesn't realize that she is overloaded; she just feels angry and cross. She screams and kicks and throws things because she can't manage any more. If we have to queue at the checkout, things really get difficult. She finds it hard to understand about taking turns. If anyone talks to us or tries to tease her in the way that some adults think is friendly, she becomes very upset. She believes everything they say. If someone says she is 'very spoilt' (a frequent comment if she is having a tantrum), she believes she is spoilt like a cake that has been cooked too long. She gets very upset and shouts at them. People frequently give me disapproving looks because of the way Jenny is behaving – even people who should know better. I know she needs to learn how to deal with things like shopping, in order to be able to manage when she grows up, but I have to be feeling really strong to even think of trying it.' (Myra)

Problems at birth

People with autism are far more likely than those who are not autistic to have had problems during their birth. For many years, it was thought that problems that occurred while a baby was being born might be the cause of autism. Children with autism tend to have larger heads than non-autistic people. When a baby is born it moves down the birth canal from its mother's womb. The birth canal is quite small and if the baby has a particularly large head, this can make it difficult to deliver the baby. Some people still believe that problems like this during the birth of the baby are responsible for autistic brain development. However, recent studies have concluded that the baby itself plays a part in the delivery process and that it may be developmental problems of the baby in the womb which lead to difficulties with delivery.

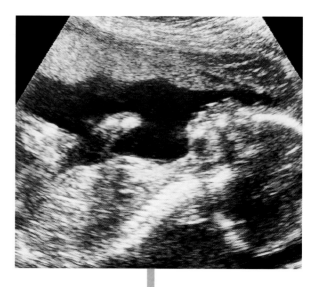

In the womb
The way a baby develops in the mother's womb can affect what happens during the birth.

Brain studies

The brain is a highly complex organ. Its many different areas are responsible for different actions, such as making sense of the sounds detected by our ears, interpreting the information gathered by our eyes (sight), and very many others. It is only within the last few years that researchers have begun to understand which parts of the brain are affected by autism. Recent studies have found changes in several areas of the brain, including the limbic system and the frontal lobes.

The limbic system is in the centre of the brain and is made up of several different structures including the hippocampus and the amygdala. The limbic system is thought to act by sorting through information received by the brain, such as sight, sound, touch, taste and smell, and enhancing the most important bits. For example, if you are in a crowded disco, your limbic system will help you hear your friend asking what you want to drink by enhancing the pieces of information relating to your friend speaking whilst not enhancing all the other sounds, flashing lights, smells, and the closeness of other dancers. It then relays this information to other areas of the brain, adding an emotional feel to the information as appropriate. It has been found that monkeys who have brain damage to their limbic system display autistic behaviour.

Recent studies have found that nerve cells in the hippocampus and amygdala in people with autism are often immature and have not gone through the usual stages of development. The amygdala is involved in controlling aggression and emotions and in responding to stimuli such as sound, sights, smells and fear.

The hippocampus plays a major role in the way our memories work. People with damage to the hippocampus have difficulty in forming new memories. People with autism often have exceptionally good memories for the past and for information, but have problems with remembering speech and things that have happened recently.

It has also been found that people with autism tend to have fewer Purkinje cells in their cerebellum, and there are fewer neurones (nerve cells) connecting the Purkinje cells. The Purkinje cells are principally involved in the coordination of body movement and in your understanding of where your body is in relation to the world around it. These cells also receive a lot of input from the limbic system. People with Asperger's syndrome often have problems with controlling their movements, making them clumsy, but much more research needs to happen before we understand how all these things work together.

hypothalamus

septum   *amygdala*

hippocampus

cerebellum

The limbic system

The limbic system is a group of structures in the centre of the brain. It helps you to process information from your senses, memory and emotions.

Genetics

The problems with brain development that cause the symptoms of autism occur while the baby is growing and developing in its mother's womb. Why do these problems happen? An increasing amount of research suggests that autism has a genetic cause. Genes link up with other genes into long coils called chromosomes. These long chains of genes are the blueprint for our bodies. Chromosomes are contained in the nucleus of each cell in our bodies. They tell the cell how to develop; certain genes are switched on or off depending on the function of the cell. For example, brain cells need to work in a different way from cells in our stomachs. All the instructions for how we grow and develop are contained in our genes, which we inherit from our parents.

Chromosomes
Every cell contains chromosomes, which are made up of strings of genes. They are the blueprint that tells the cell how to function.

The first evidence that the cause of autism could be genetic came in 1971, when a study of identical twins found that, if one identical twin had autism, the other was likely to have autism in over 90 out of 100 cases. Other studies of the sisters and brothers of children with autism also showed that they were more likely to have signs of autism than children who did not have a brother or sister with autism.

Over the last few years the situation has become clearer. Lots of research has been carried out in order to 'map' all the genes in human chromosomes. This research has begun to unravel the mystery behind many illnesses and conditions, including autism. It is now thought that autism is caused by complex interactions involving from three to 15 or more genes. In 2001 researchers identified one of the genes, called WNT2, that may be involved in causing autism. Although there is a great deal more research to do, there is now hope of being able to identify all the genes involved in autism, over the next few decades.

Identical twins
Sharing the same genes makes twins identical.

The environment

Although current research suggests that autism is an inherited genetic condition, some researchers feel that genetics are not the whole story. Their idea is that certain genes may make someone more likely to develop autism; but for autism to occur, these genes may have to be 'switched on' by something in the environment. What this environmental factor may be is not clear. Some researchers think it may be an infection and others think it may be chemical. This idea would make autism similar to asthma, in that people can be genetically susceptible to develop asthma but only actually develop the condition if they are exposed to certain things in the environment. For asthma, this may be house dust mites or pet hair. In autism the environmental factors are not so clear. Some researchers suspect that a chemical called mercury may be involved. Whatever the environmental factor is (if, indeed, it really is a factor in developing autism), then it must be present all around the world as autism occurs in every society in every country.

'I think the main cause of autism is probably genetic, but we are still at a very early stage of investigating it. It is complex and there may well be an environmental trigger involved as well. It can be hard for families to come to terms with.' (John, doctor)

The MMR debate

Over the last few years there has been a lot of debate about the role of the Measles, Mumps, Rubella (MMR) vaccine that is given to babies at one year old. In 1988, a research team at the Royal Free Hospital in London wrote about a small group of children who appeared to show signs of autism a few days after receiving the MMR vaccine. The researchers said that this finding did not prove that the vaccine caused autism in children but that more research was needed. They also said that, if MMR was causing autism, this should show up as an increased number of children with autism.

Investigating the role of the MMR vaccine in autism is important. Measles and mumps, which the vaccine prevents, can be very serious childhood illnesses. One in five children who develop measles will be left with some form of disability from the disease. Before the introduction of the vaccine, many children died from measles. Now, because of worries that the vaccine may cause autism, some parents are deciding not to have their babies vaccinated. Health officials across Europe and the USA are concerned that the number of parents who are not allowing their children to be vaccinated has increased the risk of serious childhood illness.

One study looked at the number of cases of autism around the world. It found that autism had increased worldwide, in countries that did not use the MMR vaccine as well as in countries that did. The conclusion was that there was no evidence that the

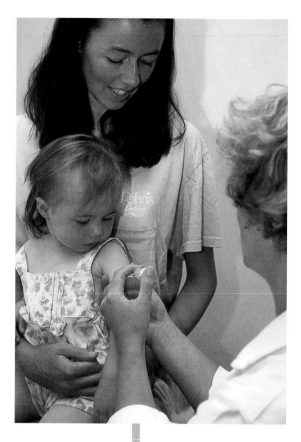

MMR jab

The Measles, Mumps, Rubella vaccine protects children from becoming ill with these diseases.

'There was no way the MMR jab had anything to do with Zac's problems. He was showing signs of them long before that.' (Kevin, dad)

MMR vaccine was causing the rise. One theory about the global rise in autistic spectrum disorders is that the number of people affected has actually remained the same; what has changed is our ability to recognize the disorders. Another theory is that something has changed in the environment.

'I'm certain MMR has something to do with my daughter's autism. There was no sign of a problem before she had the injection. A few months later she just stopped talking. The doctor says it would have started then anyway, but I'm not convinced.' (Leah)

The vast majority of research has found that the MMR vaccine is not related to autism, and yet some parents of children with an autistic spectrum disorder are convinced that it was caused by MMR. This may be because the signs of autism often only become noticeable at about 18 months old (when children normally start talking), which is also soon after the time that the MMR vaccine is given. However, parents' views should not be dismissed lightly. They love their children and are in a better position than anyone to notice changes in a child's condition. The current view of major organizations such as the National Autistic Society in Britain and many autism associations in the USA is that there is no evidence that MMR vaccine causes autism. Nonetheless, all the organizations feel that more research is needed to investigate the reasons for the rise in the numbers of people with autistic spectrum disorders around the world.

In the next chapter we will look at the different therapies and approaches that are available to help people with autism.

Measles

Measles can be a very serious illness for children.

4 Therapies for autism
Making connections

Autism cannot be cured but there are therapies that can help people with autism to communicate. Like many other therapies, these are best started young. The most useful tool an autistic person has for making sense of the world around them is intelligence. Many people with high-functioning autism or Asperger's syndrome, who have average or high intelligence, learn strategies to overcome their problems and often manage very well as adults, with jobs and families of their own. Other people with autism may need special care throughout their lives.

Most therapies are linked with education; they are not usually prescribed by doctors as treatment. This means that therapeutic help for autism tends to stop when the person leaves school, whether the school is a special needs one or mainstream. A few programmes provide social support for adults with autism who are able to live in the community. These are mostly befriending schemes designed to help prevent individuals with autism from becoming socially isolated.

'Since she started at her social skills group Jules has become much more aware of how to behave in social situations.'
(Maria, social worker)

Just as there is a wide variety of problems associated with autism, there is also a wide variety of therapies. This chapter investigates the most common therapies and how they work.

Diet and vitamins

Diet is a controversial therapy for autism. Some doctors think that this therapy may help some people with autism, particularly those whose autistic behaviour has not appeared until around two years old. They feel that some children with autism may have a condition called 'leaky gut'. If you have a 'leaky gut', food that is usually kept inside the digestive system until it is broken down into harmless substances can 'leak' into your bloodstream. This may be related to autistic behaviours and attention deficit disorder. Some people report that diets that exclude gluten (present in foods containing wheat flour) and dairy products (milk, cheese, yoghurt, cream) can help reduce autistic behaviour in some children. More research is needed before we will know for sure whether diet can affect some people with autism.

'The gluten-free diet has made a huge difference – he's sleeping better and has fewer tantrums. I know of people where it hasn't made any difference, but Jazz had bowel problems as well as autism and I've heard that the diet works better for children like him.' (Lorna)

Vitamin therapy has been better researched. In the USA in the 1960s Dr Bernard Rimland investigated the effects of vitamin B6 and magnesium on children with autism. He found that a number of them benefited with a reduction in the intensity of their behavioural problems. It seems that vitamin B6 and magnesium may help some children with autistic spectrum disorders, but only those who are deficient in B6. Another vitamin that has proved helpful for some people with autism is vitamin C. Deficiency in vitamin C causes confusion and depression among other things. It seems that vitamin C plays a part in keeping our brains working properly, but how is not yet properly understood.

'We've been trying Larrs with B6 for some time. I think it has helped a bit – it's not a cure but he doesn't seem to have as many tantrums as he used to.' (Craig)

Applied behaviour analysis

Applied behaviour analysis is a method of teaching which is often used to help children with autistic spectrum disorders. The idea is that everyone learns skills more easily if they are rewarded for their achievements. In the past, applied behaviour analysis involved being rewarded for doing the right thing and punished for doing the wrong thing. However, over the years, punishing people has not been found to be effective, whereas rewarding them is often very effective.

Achievement
Rewards of time spent doing a favourite activity can help children learn new skills.

In applied behaviour analysis, tasks are broken down into tiny achievable units. These are then taught in a structured way, so that the individual gradually builds up the skills needed to complete the whole task. Each step is rewarded with something pleasurable, such as a tiny bite of food or play with a favourite toy. With autistic people, it is very important to check that the rewards are appropriate. For example, clapping or shouting 'well done' would probably be experienced as a punishment. Once learnt, the skills are practised to ensure that the individual continues to be able to use them. Applied behaviour analysis can be used to help a child develop a single skill (such as cleaning their teeth), or many skills in a specially devised programme such as 'Lovaas'.

'Teeth cleaning was a big problem for Philip, so we broke it down into small sections. We started with going to the bathroom without a fuss and every time he achieved it, he was allowed time playing with his favourite train.'
(Peter, dad)

Working in the USA in the 1960s and '70s, Dr O. Ivar Lovaas first devised a programme based on behaviour

Applied behaviour analysis

In brief, this therapy involves:

- ◉ *breaking skills down into tiny achievable units;*
- ◉ *rewarding achievement (making sure the reward is appropriate);*
- ◉ *ignoring inappropriate behaviour and guiding towards more acceptable behaviour.*

analysis, which was used with autistic children living in residential care who had little speech. He concentrated on speech and was very successful. Dr Lovaas went on to develop a system of therapy that covered all aspects of daily living, speech and social interaction. The current Lovaas programme starts between the ages of 2 and 4 years. Children have 40 hours of structured therapy every week from trained therapists, on a one-to-one basis. Parents continue the therapy at home.

Results published in 1987 showed that 47 per cent of autistic children who followed the programme were able to enter full-time mainstream education. Another 40 per cent displayed substantial progress, whilst 10 per cent showed little or no improvement. A follow-up study in 1993 showed that the majority of the children had maintained their improvement. The therapy can be very effective, but it does have some drawbacks. It is very expensive: each child needs three trained full-time therapists for four to five years. The therapy needs to be started before the child is 5 years old, ideally before they are 3½ years old. It is also very difficult to tell which children will benefit from the therapy before you start. Another more fundamental problem with the technique is that children with autism are not able to generalize, so a skill learnt in one situation may not be used in another situation where it would be useful.

'Jasmine started with being rewarded for making a sound when she wanted a biscuit. Gradually we encouraged her to make more appropriate sounds until she built up the whole word. It's wonderful to hear her speak.'
(Nan, therapist)

Speech therapy

Verbal and non-verbal communication can be very difficult for children with autistic spectrum disorders. They can have problems speaking as well as understanding what someone is saying. Speech therapists can help children with autism to learn these things, to make sense of the verbal and non-verbal information around them. Speech and language therapists can help with every aspect of communication. Sometimes they are the first to notice that a child may have an autistic spectrum disorder. They can help children learn to speak, to communicate, and to make contact with other people – whether using their voice or another method such as pictures (see PECS system, on page 42). Autism is a profoundly isolating condition and speech therapists specialize in helping people to communicate, to share their thoughts, words and feelings.

'It's hard to look at other people's eyes. I don't like people looking at me, so I look in a different place. It makes me feel funny.'
(David, aged 10)

Speech therapists work in a variety of ways. They may work one-to-one with a client, or in small groups, or they may act as advisors to other therapists or teachers working with an individual. For autistic people with fluent speech whose main problems are with understanding what is said to them and interpreting the social aspects of communication, speech therapists tend to help mainly by giving advice. They can suggest techniques and games to help improve listening skills and understanding of body language.

For example, one useful idea is to build up a scrapbook of pictures of people expressing different feelings. It may help to take photos of familiar people, as these will be more relevant, or the pictures could be cut out of magazines. The scrapbook can then be used to play various games such as 'guess the feeling' or 'match the expression to the emotion'. Other games could involve guessing what may have happened to cause the emotion. All these games involve thinking about how other people experience the world.

Speech therapists can also help improve eye contact, and with understanding the subtle changes in tone and emphasis that change the meaning of a sentence. Eye contact can be a particular problem for people with autism. They do not understand that communication depends to a large degree on watching the speaker's face and body. Gentle teasing can sound very unkind if you do not see the facial expression with the words. Speech therapists can help improve eye contact with games such as the mind-reading game and 'Silent snap'. This involves playing a game of snap and, instead of saying 'snap' when you see two cards match, making eye contact with the other player. The game is also useful for learning about turn-taking.

The mind-reading game

This game involves guessing what another person is thinking about by watching their eye movements. If you are asked to think about an object you can see, your eyes will automatically rest briefly on the object you choose. So, by closely watching another person's eye movements, you can work out what they are thinking about. This game can help improve eye contact but is very difficult if you have autism.

Learning to communicate
A speech therapist helps autistic students to use pictures and symbols to communicate.

PECS system

For people with severe problems, speech therapists start work with teaching associations between pictures or symbols and objects. The Picture Exchange Communication System (PECS) was developed in the USA. The idea is that children are taught to exchange pictures or symbols for the objects they represent. (Many autistic children find symbols easier than pictures.) Two adults are needed at the beginning, one to hold the object (for example, an apple) and one to physically prompt the child to exchange the apple picture or symbol for the real thing. Eventually the child learns to exchange the picture or symbol for the object.

The aim is for the child to understand that the picture or symbol represents an object. Success means that a child who may not be able to speak can ask for a toy by pointing to its picture/symbol. This can be a great, exciting achievement.

If a child with autism is able to understand symbols and pictures, it is worth using them as much as possible. Symbols can help communication even for people with autism who are able to speak. They find them much easier and quicker to understand. Symbols can be used in every aspect of life. Visual timetables are especially helpful and reassuring.

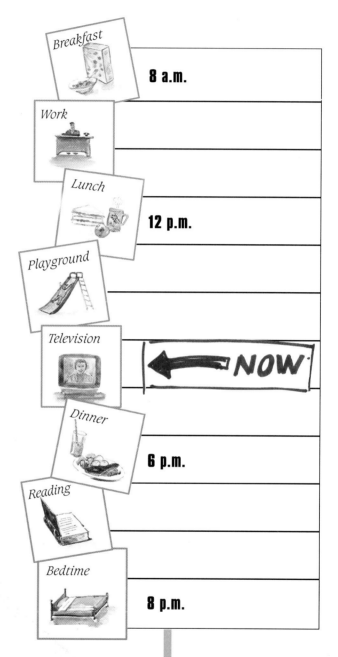

Breakfast — 8 a.m.

Work

Lunch — 12 p.m.

Playground

Television — ← NOW

Dinner — 6 p.m.

Reading

Bedtime — 8 p.m.

Visual timetable

Visual timetables use pictures or symbols of what is going to happen. They are reassuring for a person with autism.

Music therapy

Music therapy has been used to help children with autism for many years. Babies with autism often pay more attention to music than to spoken words, and it is thought that music can stimulate and develop communication in some people with autism. In order to produce music you have to be aware of yourself and aware of other people. Music therapists help develop this awareness in people with autism by using sounds. Music therapists usually work one-to-one. They may give a child an instrument to play with and, when the child makes a sound with it, respond with the same sound, or develop a rhythm. Music therapy does not involve teaching a child to play an instrument, though an appreciation of music may develop from it. For some children with autism music therapy may help to reduce sensitivity to sound. For others it may help them learn about turn-taking, listening and responding to other people and expressing themselves. There is little research into music therapy and autism but many case studies have found it to be helpful and enjoyable.

A music therapist

'I've been working in music therapy for about ten years. I started out in percussion – drums, bells, cymbals, anything you can shake or hit to make a noise. I have a degree in music and I also work as a music teacher. With autistic children, it's not learning to play a tune, or about technique. It's about sound and the rhythms that run through our lives. A child with autism may not be interested in the world around them, but they can still hear their own heart beat. That's where I usually start, tap … tap … tap … If they make a sound, then I copy it. The child is the leader, creating their own rhythms. It's fascinating. I love it when they first notice the sound, take an interest. It's like a light bulb going on.'
(Jona)

Auditory integration therapy

Sensitivity to certain sounds can be very disabling for people with autistic spectrum disorders. For example, loud unexpected sounds, electrical noises or shrill sounds can cause extreme distress. Auditory integration therapy is a new and controversial therapy for sound sensitivity. Developed by Dr G. Berard in France, the therapy involves listening to music that has been altered so that the different sound frequencies occur in a random way. The music is played at a constant volume that is loud but not painful. The trainee listens to it through headphones for half an hour, twice a day, for ten days. Dr Berard feels that auditory integration training may help autistic people 'tune in' to sounds, and thus make it easier for them to make sense of information that comes to them through their ears. No real research has been done to assess whether this therapy helps or how long its effects last.

Dolphin therapy
Swimming with dolphins is very relaxing. In dolphin therapy it is often used as a reward for learning new skills.

Daily life therapy (Higashi)

Daily life therapy was devised by Dr Kiyo Kitahara of Japan. The therapy is holistic, which means it is concerned with the whole child rather than concentrating on their difficulties. Children at Higashi schools are encouraged to develop close relationships with their therapists and the programme includes daily living skills, social skills and vigorous exercise. The education programme includes academic activities, learning to play instruments, art therapy and art appreciation. There seems to be little research on the outcome for children with autism but many parents report positive results.

SPELL

The SPELL technique has been developed over years of working with autistic children in the schools run by the National Autistic Society in the UK. SPELL stands for Structure, Positive attitudes, Empathy, Low arousal, Links.

This therapy aims to reduce the negative effects of autism and support children with autistic spectrum disorders by providing an ideal learning environment.

- 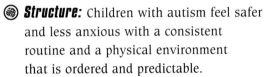 **Structure:** Children with autism feel safer and less anxious with a consistent routine and a physical environment that is ordered and predictable.

- **Positive attitudes:** This is about enhancing a child's self-esteem and confidence by making sure that targets are attainable and by building on strengths.

- **Empathy:** This involves seeing the world from each individual child's point of view, understanding their needs and providing a programme to meet them.

- **Low arousal:** This includes providing a calm, tidy, organized environment, to encourage relaxation, and using physical exercise to help relieve tension.

- **Links:** This involves linking subjects, professionals and parents and relations in order to extend each child's learning experience in an individual way.

SPELL is still being developed and researched and is used mainly in British centres for children with autism.

'It's such a relief. We were really worried moving from a mainstream school to a special school. But it has made a huge difference. He is much more relaxed and the teachers really seem to know about autism.' (Jane)

Teaching children with autism

'Normal milestones – like starting to play together or saying their first word – are far more exciting with autistic children, because they have had to work so hard to get there. It is wonderful to see them grow and start to want to be with you rather than on their own. Sometimes there is no improvement for ages. It's also hard if they start hurting each other or, worse, themselves. Sometimes we have to give parents the news that their child is more disabled than we thought. But some children manage to get back into mainstream school and that's lovely. You have to work on each individual child's level, try to see what the world looks like from their perspective.'
(Gwen, teacher at special needs school)

TEACCH

TEACCH stands for Treatment and Education of Autistic and related Communication Handicapped Children. It was started in 1966 by the Department of Psychiatry at the University of North Carolina in the United States. TEACCH focuses on helping people with autism and their families to live together by reducing autistic behaviour. The system does this by:

- *Improving adaptation:* This involves helping the autistic person to develop skills and changing their environment to minimize difficulties.

- *Parent collaboration:* Parents are trained and treated as 'co-therapists' so that the programme can be continued at home.

- *Assessment for individualized treatment:* Each person's abilities are assessed regularly and an individual educational programme is devised for them.

- *Structured teaching:* The child is taught in a structured and organized environment, to reduce anxiety.

- *Skill enhancement:* The programme focuses on developing skills that are beginning to emerge.

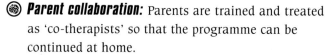

'We use toys in containers that the children cannot open on their own. They gradually learn that other people can help them to get to the toy. It helps the children to learn the value of communication.' (Terry, TEACCH therapist)

- *Cognitive therapy and behaviour therapy:* These are methods used by psychologists to help people with anxiety and other psychological difficulties to overcome their problems. TEACCH uses the therapies to help understand and improve the individual child's behaviour.

- *Generalist training:* The therapists concentrate on the whole child rather than using specialized therapies such as speech therapy or music therapy.

The TEACCH programme is more common in the USA than Britain, but many schools across the world use parts of the programme for children with autistic spectrum disorders.

Social stories

Social stories are an idea developed by Carol Gray, a teacher in the USA. They have proved very helpful, particularly for more able children with autistic spectrum disorders. The idea is that social behaviour is taught by means of a story, which can be read and re-read. Each story provides all the information needed about how to behave appropriately in a particular social situation. It tells the listener who, what, why, where, when and how. To help the person understand the social situation from different perspectives, the stories use four types of sentence: descriptive (saying what happens), directive (telling what the person should do in the situation), perspective (how other people may feel about the situation) and control (strategies the individual can use to remember what to do in the situation). Stories can be created to help individuals with autism learn how to manage in any social situation.

Steve is angry that John bumped into him.

Steve and John talk and they both feel much happier.

It's OK now.

Just look where you are going.

It hurts when someone bumps into you. It can make you feel angry. If you bump into another person it can help them to feel less angry if you say sorry and show concern for how they are feeling.

John bumps into Steve in the playground.

5 Living with autism
Family and friends

Autism can affect all areas of a person's life and the lives of those they live with. People with autism range from those needing constant care and support to those who are able to achieve independence as adults, with families of their own. However, it can take many years of patient help for someone with autism to become independent in areas that most of us take for granted.

Eating and drinking

Eating and drinking can be a problem for people with autism. They may dislike the textures and tastes of foods. They may also have problems with the smells of foods, which can make them feel overloaded and cause problems before, during and after a meal. They may have problems coordinating the muscles involved in eating. Speech therapists can use exercises to help people develop the skills they need for chewing and swallowing. These exercises include blowing bubbles and getting the person to lick their lips, by putting something sweet on them.

People with autism are often fussy eaters. Some do not seem to recognize feelings of hunger and eat very little. Others eat a small number of foods and are unwilling to try new tastes and textures. Eventually most people 'develop' out of these problems, although some continue to be fussy eaters all their life. While the problems last, it can be very difficult for the people providing food. It's important that they try not to get too upset, as anxiety can make the problems worse. The way forward can be very

Siblings
Brothers and sisters often play an important part in the day-to-day help needed by a child with an autistic spectrum disorder.

slow, but positive, quiet, gentle encouragement to eat a balanced diet can eventually help people with autism to eat the variety of food they need to stay healthy.

Washing and personal hygiene

Motivation is often a problem when it comes to bathing. Many people with autistic spectrum disorders do not care whether they become independent or not and they are unconcerned about how they look or smell to other people. It can be difficult to persuade them to learn how to wash and dress themselves. However, by breaking the skills down into small achievable goals, and with patience, positive quiet encouragement and a motivating reward system, it is possible to make progress. Once washing and dressing have become routine, the person can often be relied on to continue with this, with some supervision. People with autistic spectrum disorders love routine; it helps them feel safe and in control. Washing routines can be very useful, although sometimes they can go too far. Occasionally, people with autistic spectrum disorders develop obsessive hand washing, or special fears of washing. Particular dislikes often centre on hair washing, cutting or brushing. Your head is a very sensitive area if you have autism. The lightest touch can be experienced as pain.

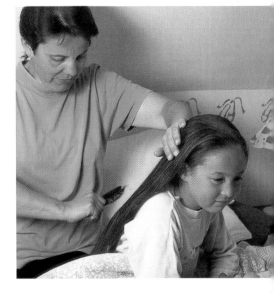

Desensitization

'Lucy always had trouble with her hair. From a tiny baby she would scream if anyone tried to touch her head. The psychologist at the hospital suggested we tried a gradual desensitization programme. We set very small targets and gradually increased them. The first target was to get Lucy to tolerate my hand gently on her head for a few seconds while she was watching her favourite video. Eventually she could manage for a few seconds. Then we extended the time slowly and gradually introduced a soft hairbrush. It took about six months altogether. Some days were better than others, but now she lets me brush her hair gently. Next we will start on hair washing.' (Karen, Lucy's mother)

Sleeping

Sleeping is a common problem for people with autism. Some children with autism never seem to develop a 'normal' sleeping cycle. Even with a strict bedtime routine, they may lie awake for long periods, be fearful of sleeping, and wake during the night and shout out. They often seem to require very little sleep. This can be true for people right across the autistic spectrum and can be exhausting and difficult to live with. Medication can help occasionally but does not help in the long term. Some people with autism are resistant to sleeping medicine and others react to it by becoming very active and restless. Regular physical exercise can help, and sometimes these problems suddenly get better as the individual gets older. Sleeping little is less of a problem for adults with autism, as they are often able to occupy themselves for the time they are awake in the night.

Help with sleeping problems

The following ideas can help when an autistic person has sleeping problems. Don't expect miracles. Measure success in small goals.

- *Keep a sleep diary, to help you work out what the problem is.*
- *Make sure that the person is not having caffeine or sugar near bedtime.*
- *Use relaxation techniques – e.g. gentle massage, aromatherapy.*
- *Reduce the stimulation in the house an hour before bedtime – reduce sound, turn the TV off.*
- *Lots of exercise during the day.*
- *Keep to a set evening routine.*
- *Make sure that the bed is comfortable – check out textures of clothing, smells, sounds. Sometimes a heavy sensation can be relaxing, so blankets may be better than quilts.*
- *Make sure the light level is right. Some people find the dark scary and need to have lights on; others are better with blackout blinds and no light.*
- *Make a visual bedtime timetable. Include information on what to do if you wake in the middle of the night.*

Movement

Movement is affected in different ways for individuals across the autistic spectrum. Some people with autism are very agile and fearless (which can be nerve-wracking); some are restless, pacing up and down or fidgeting. Others, particularly those with high-functioning autism and Asperger's syndrome, tend to be clumsy; they may hold their hands stiffly when running and they may walk with their head and shoulders bent forward. Despite this difficulty in controlling big movements, they can have good coordination of some fine movements, especially if a special interest requires a lot of hand control. Clumsy movements can be helped by exercises focusing on balance and by increasing a child's awareness of their body. Crawling around on the floor can help, as can activities like swimming and trampolining.

Horse-riding

Horse-riding is often used as a therapy for people with autism. It helps develop balance and coordination and is enjoyable.

Children with autism often do repetitive movements called 'stereotypies'. These include hand flapping, finger rolling, rocking, and jumping up and down on the spot. Excitement, anger and anxiety tend to make these movements more obvious, whereas they tend to disappear if the individual is concentrating on something they find interesting. These movements can persist through childhood into adult life. If a person with autism is asked to stop doing these movements, they can become upset and agitated. It is better to ignore the movements as

'I find the noises and movements embarrassing. They're worse in public places. They're better if he's holding something he likes. Game boys are the best – as long as you can persuade him to turn down the sound.'
(Toby, whose brother has Asperger's)

much as possible or to make sure an interesting distraction is available for times when they are particularly inappropriate or embarrassing (hand-held electronic games can be very useful distracters). Exercise is particularly helpful, as it can help reduce aggressive behaviour and reduce stereotypies as well as improve general health.

Avoiding tantrums

Tantrums involve a sometimes violent outburst in response to stress. The individual may lie on the floor and scream, throw things and generally lose control in rage. Tantrums are part of normal behaviour for all young children, who frequently go through a stage of having tantrums around the age of two or three. For people with autism tantrums can continue to be a problem right through childhood and, in some cases, throughout their life, although for many people the tantrums gradually disappear at the end of adolescence. Tantrums can be particularly difficult for friends and siblings to manage or understand.

'My mate Ryan has tantrums sometimes, when things get too much for him. He punches and screams and breaks things. I try to get out of the way when he's like that.' (Andy, aged 14)

When anyone is under stress they tend to be grumpy and irritable. People with autism are just the same, but they experience more stress than other people. They are constantly bombarded by stimulation, anxiety and change; and they have less social embarrassment than other people about losing their temper. It can be helpful to try to find out the causes of the tantrums. Certain types of sounds or smells or groups of people can make tantrums more likely and are best avoided. Change, which can be as small as moving a treasured possession, can also provoke an outburst. Remaining calm and firm, with a quiet voice, is the best approach. Ignore the tantrum as long as the individual is not in danger. Consistency is important and everyone involved in caring for the person needs to agree on how to respond.

'Toni has times when he loses control. They were hard to manage when he was younger and since he reached 13 they seem to be getting bad again. I've heard this can happen when you have autism.' (Keith, dad)

Encouraging communication

'We have several children with Asperger's syndrome at this school. As a rule, they are very law-abiding and little trouble. In fact, it is very easy, I think, to underestimate how difficult they are finding school. Certainly some of the children we have do not display their anxiety at school. They appear to be coping most of the time, but can become very distressed when they get home. It took me a while to grasp this idea. If teachers are not seeing signs of distress at school, they can easily assume that tantrums at home are nothing to do with them. Now I realize that children with autistic spectrum disorders take a while to process what happens at school. They may not react to anxiety, which started at school, until many hours later. We now have a policy of encouraging parents to let us know about any anxieties that may be building up, so we can nip the problem in the bud.'
(Malcolm, senior school headmaster)

Taking an interest

Sensitive support at school can help reduce the amount of anxiety experienced by autistic people.

People with high-functioning autism and Asperger's syndrome are also prone to tantrums. These can be a problem at school where other students soon pick up on the fact that the person is different and easy to tease. Young people with high-functioning autism and Asperger's syndrome quickly become distressed by teasing and can lose control aggressively. Because they find it hard to understand how others are feeling, they may not control their response and can be violent, which gets them into trouble. However, strategies for self-control, such as counting to ten before you act, deep breathing and avoidance strategies, can be helpful in reducing these outbursts as the individual grows older.

School and college

People with autism get on best in environments that are stable, supportive, structured, consistent, well-organized and predictable. People with severe autism may need to live permanently in residential schools. Those who find it difficult to cope in mainstream schools may need to attend special schools until they learn the skills they need to manage in mainstream. Many people with high-functioning autism and Asperger's syndrome manage well in mainstream schools, with support. However, the number of people, noise level and variety of activities can cause severe anxiety.

Between lessons
In a noisy corridor it is reassuring for an autistic student to have the company and support of a friend.

Social situations

People with autistic spectrum disorders need extra support in social situations. They find it hard to understand hierarchy and this, combined with their tendency to tell things as they are, can make them appear rude. They often do not realize that when the teacher is talking to the whole class, it includes them. They find it very hard to ask for help or even understand that they need help. Places like the playground and corridors between lessons are particularly difficult, due to noise and crowding. An autistic student can quickly become distressed and may be unable to tell anyone how they are feeling. This can lead to them behaving oddly, which then can lead to teasing or bullying. It is good if such a student can have a friend with them to help them respond appropriately, like having an interpreter in a foreign country. It also helps to review conversations or confrontations in a safe place, later, and to role-play different ways of responding.

Bullying

People with autistic spectrum disorders are ideal targets for bullies, and frequently suffer taunting and teasing. They may not understand what is happening and may not be able to communicate their distress about it. People with autistic spectrum disorders tend to talk about their feelings (if they do so at all) in a flat, expressionless voice, or they may show their distress by increased anxiety levels, tantrums, retreating into their special interest or becoming depressed

'Amy had been bullied for several months before we found out. They told her, if she said anything, she would be taken away. Because she takes everything literally, she believed them.'
(Alison, mum)

It can help to role-play teasing situations with the autistic person so that they can practise how to handle them. It can also help to identify behaviour that may cause the teasing. Maybe the person stands in other people's personal space, or only talks about one subject. These are social skills that may need to be learnt. People with autism do not pick these skills up naturally just by watching other people.

Change

The move from primary to secondary school or from secondary school to college can be very traumatic and challenging for people with autistic spectrum disorders. They need special understanding and support at these times. Planning the move early can help. So can visiting the new environment when no other students are there, finding out what the timetable will be like and planning strategies for managing potentially difficult situations such as class changeover times. Learning to write things down and to use lists and timetables can reduce anxiety.

The move to college can be very difficult, especially if it involves moving away from home. For some students, religious groups can provide valuable ongoing support in a structured environment. On the other hand, some people with autism are particularly vulnerable to the influence of sects, who try to recruit new members from students newly away from home. Some colleges have a mentoring system, where individuals are assigned a 'mentor' to help and advise them. This can provide essential social support and reassurance in a new environment.

Adolescence

For some children the effects of their autism change very little when they reach adolescence and these people remain dependent for the whole of their lives. Other young people with autism change so much that they are able to become independent and live a completely 'normal' adult life, though problems with social skills may continue. These problems can include brutal honesty, and intolerance of people who are not as honest as they are, as well as not knowing how to act in situations that involve emotions. For example, the autistic person may ignore or walk away from someone who is weeping. Problems noticing the social cues that tell you that someone is bored or uncomfortable often remain, as do problems making and keeping friends and working out who is a suitable friend.

'Kado is very honest – like when he told our science teacher that he had bad breath! But you really know where you stand with a friend like him. If he says something, you know he really means it. He's great!' (Sam)

Many people with autism find adolescence a very difficult time. They tend to have more tantrums and these can be harder to manage, as they are much stronger and bigger. The physical changes of adolescence occur normally but people with autism often look and behave much younger than they are. People with severe autism may not be interested in other people enough to seek out sexual partners, but most eventually discover masturbation. Then it can be difficult for them to learn that masturbation should be done in private.

For those with high-functioning autism or Asperger's syndrome the onset of adolescence is often upsetting. Bodily changes can be very distressing for people who hate change. The signs of autism can become more obvious for a while, due to the increased stress of hormones and rapid growth. The social developments of adolescence may not occur until much later than in non-autistic teenagers. For instance, some people with autism do not develop 'crushes' until they are in their twenties and for others teenage infatuations can continue into middle age or beyond.

Personal safety is a real issue for people with autism. They are very vulnerable. They take language literally and are very trusting. They find it hard to work out who can be trusted and whom it is best to avoid. Learning what to do if a stranger approaches you, or who to trust if you get lost, is very important, and very difficult if you have problems understanding social situations. People with autism are socially naive and often behave and appear younger than their years. Road safety is a particular concern as they are prone to impulsive actions, which can lead them to run out in front of cars. It is essential to learn skills like these in order to be able to live safely and independently.

Too much honesty

'I really worry for Dawn's safety sometimes. She doesn't change her behaviour depending on where she is. If she sits next to someone on the bus who has been drinking, she is likely to tell them that their breath smells: obviously not the safest conversation to have with a drunk stranger. We are working on this and they are doing some stuff about personal safety at school. You have to be so careful, though. I don't want to make her more anxious, or she may get afraid to go out at all. It's got to be a gradual learning thing.'
(Shona, Dawn's mother)

Finding a job

People with autistic spectrum disorders often have special interests that dominate their lives. These special interests have a positive side, especially if they convert easily into a work situation where the person becomes an expert at a subject.

'Working as a musician is a dream come true. I get to study music, sometimes for 14 hours a day, more sometimes. Luckily my partner is a musician too, though sometimes even he gets bored.' (Kasha, violinist, aged 28, with Asperger's syndrome)

Luckily there are a wide variety of work situations that special interests can fit into. Able people with autism often take a special interest in a particular type of machine and turn out to be excellent engineers. Computer programming is another common source of employment for people with autism who are fascinated with computers. Other areas in which people with autism often find work include art, music, science and contract law. Universities are ideal working environments for able people with autism, as individuals are valued there for their academic abilities and poor social skills are tolerated.

For people with autism who are not as able, there are other possible avenues. Work where there is a set routine, structured social interaction and a nurturing atmosphere within the company is most suitable. Record keeping and jobs that involve sorting and collating, such as postal work or work at a lost property office, are good examples. For individuals with severe autistic disability work may be impossible. Some people are so severely affected that they never learn to communicate and may need permanent support and care.

'I love the way computers work, the flow of information. They're very graphic concepts. I've written my own software programmes since I was very young. Working in software design was a logical progression.' (Shabib, software designer, aged 35, with high-functioning autism)

Relationships and having a family

Many people with autism go on to marry and have a family of their own. Sometimes they develop a relationship with someone who shares their interest and occasionally their autistic qualities. Sometimes they develop relationships with people who are very good at social relationships, such as maternal, caring people. People with autistic spectrum disorders are often good-looking (though why is not known); they often come across as the 'strong, silent, gentle' type of person and can be very attractive. Often their girlfriend or boyfriend can become their 'special interest' for a while and if you are attracted to the person, this can be very flattering.

Problems can occur after marriage when the person with autism stops trying so hard and their autistic qualities become more obvious. It can be hard to live with someone who is brutally honest, is distracted by detail and doesn't notice if you are upset. This situation can be exacerbated by the birth of children, especially if some of them have autistic disorders too. Adults with autistic spectrum disorders need to learn how to conduct relationships, just as they need to learn how to be a friend. Relationship counsellors can be a great help to get over these difficulties.

Autism can be a very difficult condition to live with, but it can also be inspirational. It can bring a unique and valuable view on life. Having a friend with autism can be very rewarding. You just have to learn how to connect.

The right connections

A friend who is autistic can add special qualities to a relationship.

Glossary

Asperger's syndrome — a disorder on the autistic spectrum, usually affecting people with average or above-average intelligence. People with Asperger's syndrome often want to make friends but find it very difficult.

autism — a disorder that involves problems with social relationships, verbal and non-verbal communication, and imagination.

autistic savant — an autistic person who, despite severe autistic disability, displays amazing talent in one particular area, such as music, maths or art.

autistic spectrum disorder — Autism is a 'spectrum disorder' because its effects vary for different people and disability can range from severe to mild.

befriending schemes — schemes, often run by charities, providing individuals to act as friends for people who are socially isolated through disease or disability.

behaviour therapy — a form of therapy that tries to change behaviour by rewarding desirable behaviour and ignoring undesirable behaviour.

chromosomes — long strands of genes present in the nucleus of a cell. There are 46 chromosomes in each human cell.

classic autism — a form of autism which usually shows around 30 months of age. The individual is withdrawn, has little interest in others, has severe communication difficulties and responds to his environment in unusual ways.

cognitive therapy — a form of therapy that aims to change how you think about something that is causing a problem. The idea is that, if you think differently, you will behave differently.

compulsive behaviours — where an individual feels compelled to perform certain behaviours, such as hand washing, over and over again.

desensitization — a method of reducing sensitivity to a stimulus.

diagnosis — a doctor's expert opinion about the name of the disease or disorder that is causing someone's problem.

empathy — awareness of the emotions and feelings of another person.

genes — parts of the genetic code present in each of your body cells and controlling how your body grows and develops. You inherit your genetic code from your parents.

genetic — to do with genes.

genetics — the scientific study of genes, their structure and function.

gluten — a protein present in wheat.

high-functioning autism — an autistic spectrum disorder affecting people who have average to above-average intelligence.

holistic — looking at the whole person. It is often used to mean looking at how something affects an individual physically, socially and psychologically.

hyperactivity being over-active, or more active than the majority of people. Hyperactive people often have problems with concentration and their behaviour.

learning difficulties problems or difficulties learning new skills.

learning disabilities disabilities that make it hard to learn new skills.

mental illness disease of the mind.

mercury a metal that is liquid at room temperature and is poisonous to humans.

obsession a fixation on something. When people are obsessed by something, they cannot stop thinking about it and seem to be unable to control their thoughts.

Pervasive Developmental Disorders a set of disorders involving problems with speech, communication and getting on with other people (social interaction), as well as repetitive and compulsive behaviours.

Purkinje cells large nerve cells found in the cerebellum area of the brain.

rigid thinking inflexible thought, keeping the same ideas no matter what evidence is presented. This kind of thinking makes it difficult for someone to be deflected from an inappropriate behaviour.

social skills the knowledge and ability to get on with people and adapt to different social situations.

spectrum disorder a disorder that encompasses several individual but similar disorders which have the same cause and vary in severity.

stereotypies behaviours or movements that are repeated over and over again.

syndrome a group of symptoms or behaviours that occur together and are related to each other.

theory of mind the knowledge that other people have minds and that they are individual people who, though sharing your environment, may experience things in different ways.

therapy a general term used to describe treatments for diseases and disorders.

vaccination a method of producing immunity to a disease by injecting a small amount of a substance that will cause the immune system to develop antibodies to the disease.

vitamin a substance present in nutritious food that is essential for normal bodily function.

X chromosome the chromosome that determines whether you will be male or female. Females have two X chromosomes and males have one X and one Y chromosome.

Resources

Books

K. Hall, *Asperger's Syndrome, the Universe and Everything* (Jessica Kingsley, 2000)
A book about Asperger's written by someone who has the condition.

K. Hoopmann, *Blue Bottle Mystery An Asperger adventure* (Jessica Kingsley, 2000)
An excellent introduction to the world as seen through the eyes of a person with Asperger's.

M. Ives and N. Munro, *Caring for a child with autism* (Jessica Kingsley, 2001)
A handbook for parents and carers from the National Autistic Society.

J. Matthews and J. Williams, *The self help guide for special kids and their parents* (Jessica Kingsley, 2000)
Written by a mother and son team (James, the son, has autism), this has a positive approach and lots of good ideas.

Films

Son-Rise a miracle of love (1979, USA) is a true story of parental love and tenacity at finding a way to communicate with their autistic son.

Forrest Gump (1994, USA). The character of Forrest Gump is not classically autistic but he does have issues with language, truthfulness and routine that are similar to autism.

Rain Man (1988, USA) is a classic tale of an 'autistic savant'. Dustin Hoffman researched his role meticulously.

A day in the death of Joe Egg (1971, UK) stars Alan Bates as a teacher who struggles to cope with the needs of his disabled daughter.

Little Voice (1998, UK). The character of Little Voice has many autistic qualities, including the ability to imitate.

Societies

Allergy Induced Autism,
11 Larklands, Longthorpe,
Peterborough PE3 6LL

Autism Society of America,
7910 Woodmount Avenue, Suite 300,
Bethesda MD 20814-3067

National Autistic Society,
393 City Road, London EC1V 1NG
General enquiries: 020 7903 3599
Helpline: 0870 600 85 85
www.nas.org.uk

OAASIS (Office for Advice, Assistance, Support and Information on Special Needs)
Brock House, Grigg Lane,
Brockenhurst, Hants SO42 7RE
www.oaasis.co.uk (this website includes very useful information sheets about autism and Asperger's)

Sources

The following were used as sources of information for this book:

Tony Attwood, *Asperger's syndrome, a guide for parents and professionals* (Jessica Kingsley, 1998)

Uta Frith, *Autism and Asperger's syndrome* (CUP, 1991)

Carol Gray, *My Social Stories Book* (Jessica Kingsley, 2002)

P. Howlin, S. Baron-Cohen, J. Hadwin, *Teaching children with autism to mind read* (John Wiley, 1999)

Lorna Wing, *The Autistic Spectrum, a guide for parents and professionals* (Constable, 1996)

Disclaimer
The website addresses (URLs) included in this book were valid at the time of going to press. However, because of the nature of the internet, it is possible that some addresses may have changed, or sites may have changed or closed down since publication. While the author and the publishers regret any inconvenience this may cause readers, no responsibility for any such changes can be accepted by either the author or the publishers.

Index